Contents

Cities, Counties, and Towns Cited in this Report

Albany, New York
Albuquerque, New Mexico
Bellingham, Washington
Boston, Massachusetts
Boulder/Boulder County, Colorado
Burlington, Vermont
Chapel Hill/Orange County, North Carolina
Chicago, Illinois
Cincinnati, Ohio
Cleveland, Ohio
Delray Beach, Florida
Duluth, Minnesota
Durham, North Carolina
Flagstaff, Arizona
Gloucester, Massachusetts
Highland Park/Moraine Township, Illinois
Irvine, California
Lawrence, Kansas
Los Angeles County, California
Madison, Wisconsin
Minneapolis/Hennepin County, Minnesota
Missoula, Montana
Orcus Island, Washington
Petaluma, California
Phoenix, Arizona
Point Reyes Station, California
Portland/Multnomah County, Oregon
Rochester, Minnesota
San Bernardino County, California
Santa Monica, California
Sarasota/Sarasota County, Florida
Seattle/King County, Washington
Syracuse, New York
Truckee, California
Washington, DC

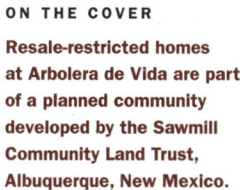

ON THE COVER

Resale-restricted homes at Arbolera de Vida are part of a planned community developed by the Sawmill Community Land Trust, Albuquerque, New Mexico.

Executive Summary

The community land trust (CLT) movement is young but expanding rapidly. Nearly 20 CLTs are started every year as either new nonprofits or as programs or subsidiaries of existing organizations. Fueling this proliferation is a dramatic increase in local government investment and involvement. Over the past decade, growing numbers of cities and counties have chosen not only to support existing CLTs, but also to start new ones, actively guiding their development and sponsoring their affordable housing initiatives.

Two key policy needs are driving this new interest in CLTs, particularly in jurisdictions that put a social priority on promoting homeownership for lower-income families and a fiscal priority on protecting the public's investment in affordable housing.

- ***Long-term preservation of subsidies.*** With local governments now assuming greater responsibility for creating affordable housing, policy makers must find ways to ensure that their investments have a sustained impact. CLT ownership of the land, along with durable affordability controls over the resale of any housing built on that land, ensures that municipally subsidized homes remain available for lower-income homebuyers for generations to come.

- ***Long-term stewardship of housing.*** Preserving affordability requires long-term monitoring and enforcement, an administrative burden that local governments are neither equipped for nor generally interested in taking on. CLTs are well positioned to play this stewardship role by administering the municipality's eligibility, affordability, and occupancy controls, while also "backstopping" lower-income owners to protect subsidized homes against loss through deferred maintenance or mortgage foreclosure.

Municipal support comes in a variety of forms, depending on how well established the CLT is. For example, local governments may offer administrative or financial support during the planning and startup phase, followed by donations of city-owned land and grants or low-interest loans for developing and financing projects. They may help a CLT acquire and preserve housing provided by private developers to comply with inclusionary zoning, density bonuses, and other mandates or concessions. As the CLT builds its portfolio, municipalities may provide capacity grants to help support its operations. Finally, local jurisdictions may assist CLTs by revising their tax assessment practices to ensure fair treatment of resale-restricted homes built on their lands.

As welcome as their support has been, local governments may inadvertently structure CLT funding and oversight in ways that undermine the effectiveness of the very model they are attempting to support. The challenge lies in finding the most constructive ways of putting municipal resources to work in pursuit of common objectives.

Troy Gardens, a project of the Madison (Wisconsin) Area Community Land Trust, integrates green-space preservation and community farming with the construction of affordable housing.

Based on a review of three dozen municipal programs and in-depth interviews with local officials and CLT practitioners, this report describes the mechanisms and methods that cities across the country are using to structure their investment in CLT startups, projects, and operations. In addition to describing the full range of options for providing municipal support, the report highlights specific model practices for rendering that assistance. These practices have the most potential to balance the interests of all parties by:

- protecting the public's investment in affordable housing;
- expanding and preserving access to homeownership for households excluded from the market;
- stabilizing neighborhoods buffeted by cycles of disinvestment or reinvestment; and
- ensuring accountability to funders, taxpayers, and the communities served by the CLT.

The city–CLT relationship continues to evolve. This report ends with a discussion of three emerging trends: shifts in the city's role from supporter to instigator, and from participant to governor; and a deepening of the CLT's primary role as a steward of affordable housing created with municipal assistance. While posing new challenges, these changes also present new opportunities for tomorrow's city–CLT partnerships.

This report is drawn from the authors' recent Lincoln Institute working paper, *Building Better City–CLT Partnerships: A Program Manual for Municipalities and Community Land Trusts*, which provides an extensive discussion of the best—and worst—ways for cities to support CLTs.

CHAPTER 1
Introducing the CLT

I n the early 1980s only a handful of community land trusts existed in the United States—nearly all located in rural areas. By 2008, more than 200 CLT programs were operating in 41 states and the District of Columbia, with a growing number of new CLTs added each year (see figure 1). Now located predominantly in cities, towns, and suburbs, these CLTs are holding land, developing housing, revitalizing neighborhoods, stewarding assets, and recapturing publicly generated value for the benefit of future generations.

HOW COMMUNITY LAND TRUSTS WORK

A community land trust is a nonprofit organization formed to hold title to land to preserve its long-term availability for affordable housing and other community uses. A land trust typically receives public or private donations of land or uses government subsidies to purchase land on which housing can be built. The homes are sold to lower-income families, but the CLT retains ownership of the land and provides long-term ground leases to homebuyers. The CLT also retains a long-term option to repurchase the homes at a formula-driven price when homeowners later decide to move (see box 1).

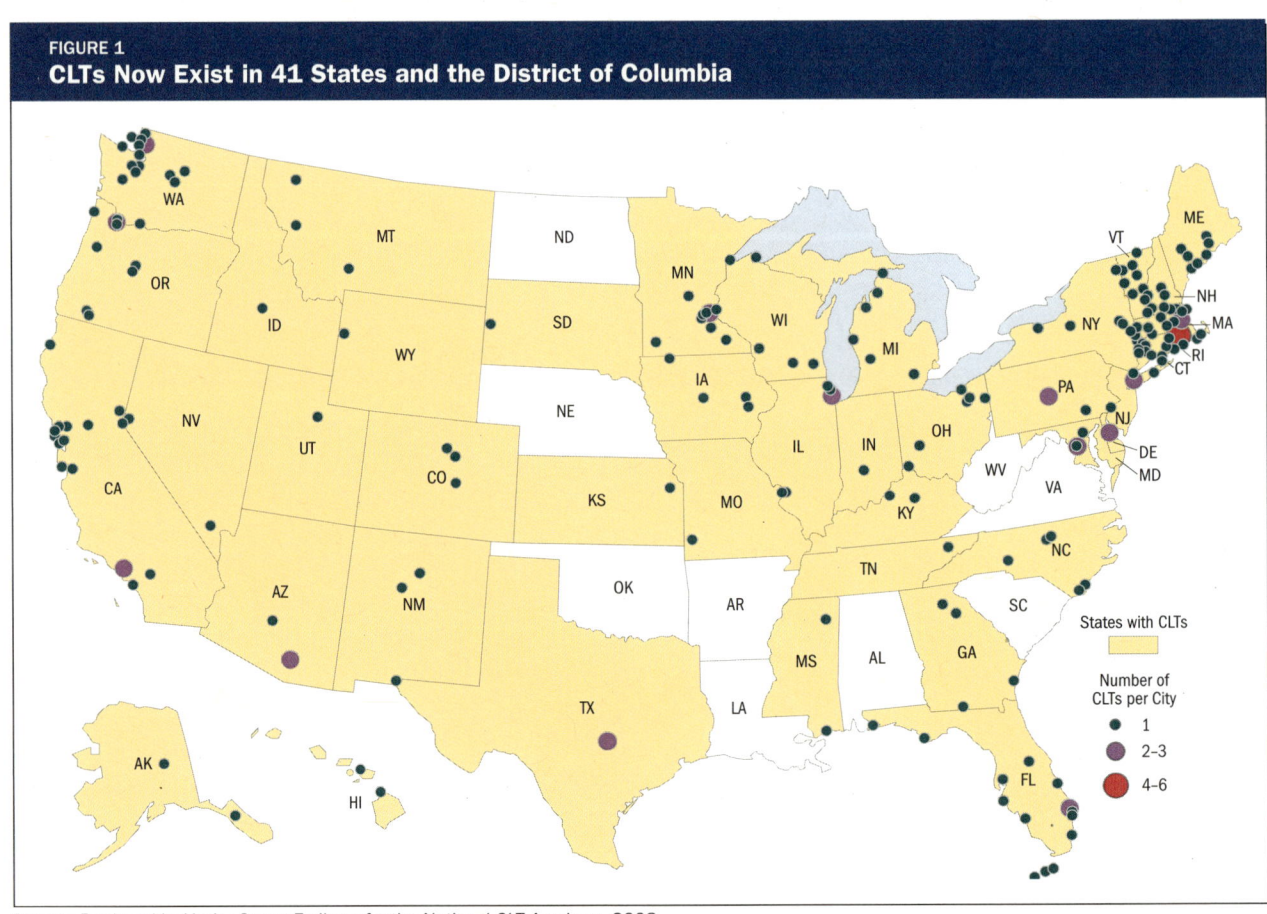

FIGURE 1
CLTs Now Exist in 41 States and the District of Columbia

Source: Produced by Yesim Sungu-Eryilmaz for the National CLT Academy, 2008.

BOX 1
Ten Key Features of the Classic Community Land Trust

1. **Nonprofit, tax-exempt corporation.** A community land trust is an independent, nonprofit corporation that is chartered in the state where it is located. Most CLTs are started from scratch, but some are grafted onto existing nonprofit corporations. Most CLTs target their activities and resources toward charitable goals such as providing housing for low-income people and redeveloping blighted neighborhoods, and are therefore eligible for 501(c)(3) designation.

2. **Dual ownership.** The CLT acquires multiple parcels of land throughout a targeted geographic area with the intention of retaining ownership permanently. The parcels do not need to be contiguous. Any buildings already located or later constructed on the land are sold to individual homeowners, condo owners, cooperative housing corporations, nonprofit developers of rental housing, or other nonprofit, governmental, or for-profit entities.

3. **Leased land.** CLTs provide for the exclusive use of their land by the owners of any buildings located thereon. Parcels of land are conveyed to individual homeowners (or the owners of other types of residential or commercial structures) through long-term ground leases.

4. **Perpetual affordability.** By design and by intent, the CLT is committed to preserving the affordability of housing and other structures on its land. The CLT retains an option to repurchase any structures located upon its land if their owners choose to sell. The resale price is set by a formula in the ground lease providing current owners a fair return on their investments and future buyers fair access to housing at an affordable price.

5. **Perpetual responsibility.** As the owner of the underlying land and of an option to repurchase any buildings located on that land, the CLT has an abiding interest in what happens to these structures and to the people who occupy them. The ground lease requires owner-occupancy and responsible use of the premises. If buildings become hazardous, the CLT has the right to force repairs. If property owners default on their mortgages, the CLT has the right to cure the default, forestalling foreclosure.

6. **Open, place-based membership.** The CLT operates within the boundaries of a targeted area. It is guided by, and accountable to, the people who call this locale their home. Any adult who resides on the CLT's land or within the area the CLT deems as its "community" can become a voting member. The community may comprise a single neighborhood, multiple neighborhoods, or even an entire town, city, or county.

7. **Community control.** Voting members who either live on the CLT's land or reside in the CLT's targeted area nominate and elect two-thirds of a CLT's board of directors.

8. **Tripartite governance.** The board of directors of the classic CLT has three parts, each with an equal number of seats. One-third represents the interests of people who lease land from the CLT; one-third represents the interests of residents of the surrounding community who do not lease CLT land; and one-third is made up of public officials, local funders, nonprofit providers of housing or social services, and other individuals presumed to speak for the public interest.

9. **Expansionist program.** CLTs are committed to an active acquisition and development program that is aimed at expanding their holdings of land and increasing the supply of affordable housing and other structures under their stewardship.

10. **Flexible development.** While land is always the key ingredient, the types of projects that CLTs pursue and the roles they play in developing the projects vary widely. Many CLTs do development with their own staff, while others delegate this responsibility to partners. Some focus on a single type and tenure of housing, while others develop housing of many types and tenures. Other CLTs focus more broadly on comprehensive community development.

Source: Davis (2007)

The "classic" CLT balances the multiple interests of homeowners, neighborhood residents, and the city as a whole in serving as the steward for an expanding stock of permanently affordable, owner-occupied housing. Homeowners leasing and living on the CLT's land (leaseholder representatives), residents of the CLT's service area (general representatives), and individuals representing the public interest (which may include municipal officials) each make up a third of a typical board of directors. This tripartite structure ensures that different land-based interests will be heard, with no single set of interests allowed to dominate.

On an operational level, CLTs take on a range of responsibilities for developing and stewarding their lands. Some focus on creating only homeownership units, while others take advantage of the model's flexibility to develop rental housing, mobile home parks, commercial space, and other community facilities. Most CLTs initiate and oversee development projects with their own staff, but others confine their efforts to assembling land and preserving the affordability of any buildings located upon it.

In their capacity as stewards, CLTs provide the oversight necessary to ensure that subsidized units remain affordable, that occupants are income-eligible, and that units are kept in good repair. Because they retain permanent ownership of the land under housing and other structural improvements, CLTs are closely connected to the homes and to the households that live in them. And as the landowner, the CLT collects a modest monthly ground lease from every homeowner, allowing the CLT to monitor its assets, protect its investment, and support residents who experience financial difficulties.

Although specific stewardship roles differ from one community to the next, nearly every CLT performs the following tasks:

- assembling and managing land;
- ensuring that owner-occupied homes remain affordably priced;
- marketing the homes through a fair and transparent process;
- educating prospective buyers about the rights and responsibilities of owning a resale-restricted home;
- selecting income-eligible buyers for the homes;
- monitoring and enforcing homeowner compliance with contractual controls over the occupancy, subletting, financing, repair, and improvement of their homes;
- verifying that homeowners maintain property insurance and pay all taxes;
- managing resales to ensure that homes are transferred to other income-eligible households for no more than the formula-determined price; and
- intervening in cases of a homeowner's mortgage default.

Most CLTs initially rely on grants from local governments, private foundations, or other donors to pay for stewardship functions. As its portfolio of land and resale-restricted housing expands, however, the CLT can generate ground lease fees, resale fees, and other income to support the costs of managing the affordable housing stock. With growth, the revenues available for stewardship also increase, allowing the CLT to make a permanent commitment to monitoring and supporting homes located on its land.

HOW CLTS EXPAND HOMEOWNERSHIP

Many municipalities have long operated homeownership programs that provide direct assistance to lower-income buyers. This approach usually involves either an outright grant or a no-interest or deferred-interest loan—typically structured as a second mortgage—to reduce monthly mortgage payments to the point where the buyer can afford to purchase a market-priced home.

The CLT model is built around a different approach that uses the same subsidy—typically given to the CLT rather than to the homebuyer—to reduce the purchase price of the home to an affordable level. Over the long term, the effect of the two approaches differs dramatically. The traditional subsidy temporarily creates affordable payments, while the CLT model permanently creates affordable housing.

In real estate markets where housing prices rise faster than household incomes, the level of traditional subsidy that each successive homebuyer needs to afford market-priced housing increases steadily (see figure 2a). Even if homeowners are required to repay most or even all of the subsidy when they sell, an additional subsidy is usually necessary to fill the affordability gap that continues to widen during their occupancy (see figure 2b). The next generation of lower-income buyers is likely to need far larger subsidies than those required to lift the first households into homeownership.

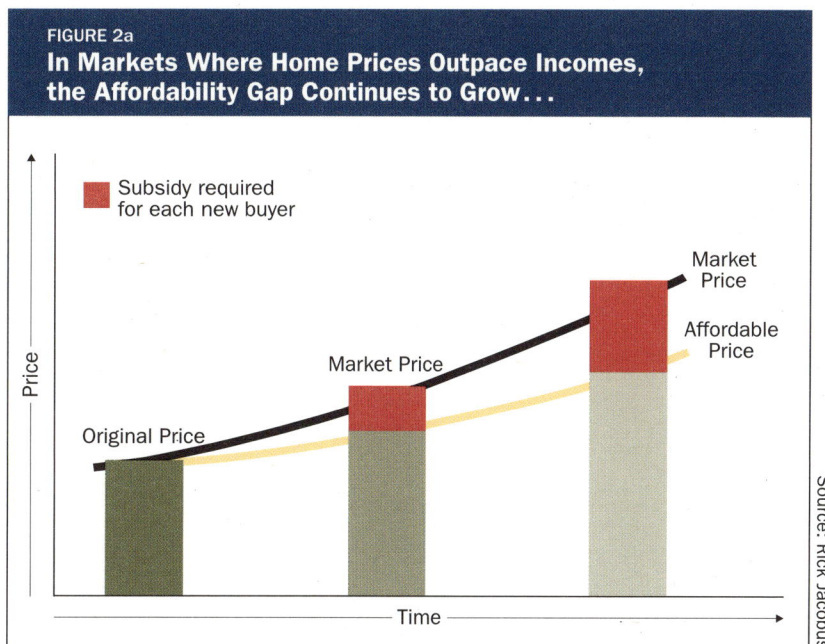

FIGURE 2a
In Markets Where Home Prices Outpace Incomes, the Affordability Gap Continues to Grow...

Source: Rick Jacobus

If housing prices rise faster than household incomes, the affordability gap widens. As a result, it takes an ever-larger subsidy to keep a home affordable. Programs providing loans or grants to homebuyers must constantly increase the level of subsidy to keep pace with the growing gap between market and affordable prices.

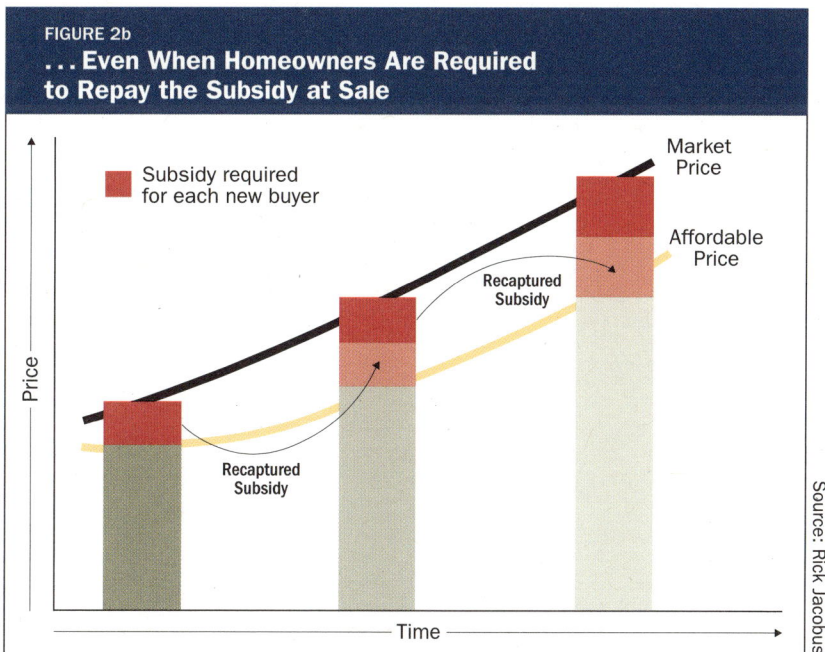

FIGURE 2b
...Even When Homeowners Are Required to Repay the Subsidy at Sale

Source: Rick Jacobus

Recapturing the original subsidy and reinvesting it in new loans to other lower-income households does not prevent the affordability gap from growing. An ever-larger subsidy is still needed to help subsequent generations of homebuyers if prices continue to rise faster than incomes.

The CLT strategy, in contrast, is to invest in creating a stock of permanently affordable, owner-occupied housing (see figure 3). The CLT uses the public (and private) funds to acquire land and perhaps to cover other costs of housing development. As a result, it can sell homes at prices that lower-income households can afford without a second loan or other special financing. If they decide to move, the initial buyers must sell the subsidized homes for a formula-driven price that other lower-income homebuyers can afford. By maintaining ownership of land across multiple sales of the house, the CLT can usually keep homes affordable for many years without the need for additional infusions of public capital. But because it cannot control other factors that influence housing costs—such as rising insurance or utility costs, property taxes, and/or mortgage interest rates—no CLT can absolutely guarantee it will never need an additional subsidy. It can, however, assure its municipal partner that any further subsidy will always be substantially less than what would be required without the CLT's resale controls.

Table 1 compares the performance of two types of subsidies: (1) a homebuyer loan in the form of a silent second mortgage where the funds are to be repaid at resale without interest; and (2) a CLT subsidy in which the resale price may not exceed the initial (affordable) purchase price plus an adjustment based on the annual change in the area median income (AMI). The home is assumed to have a value of $250,000 in a market where a family in the target income range can afford to pay only $200,000.

Bridging the affordability gap at the time of initial sale entails a $50,000 subsidy regardless of the option selected. When the first owner sells, however, the two approaches differ in how well they preserve the value of the public investment and how large a return the seller realizes on his/her investment. The first homebuyer's net proceeds following the sale in the

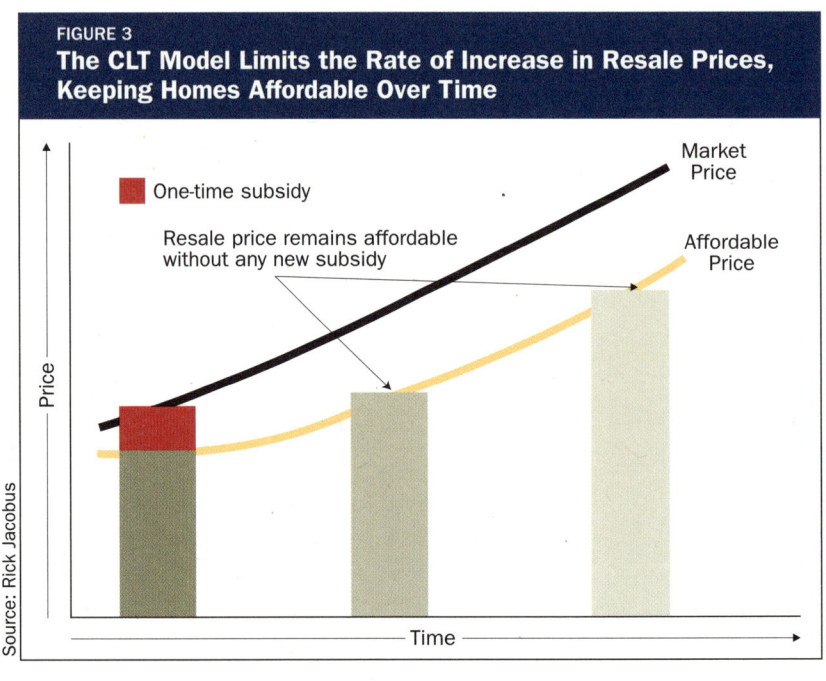

FIGURE 3
The CLT Model Limits the Rate of Increase in Resale Prices, Keeping Homes Affordable Over Time

Market Price

One-time subsidy

Resale price remains affordable without any new subsidy

Affordable Price

Price

Time

Source: Rick Jacobus

A one-time subsidy in a CLT home lowers its initial sale price to an affordable level and then limits the rate at which the price can rise over time. This strategy helps to increase the stock of permanently affordable housing.

seventh year are greatest under the loan program, although the CLT-subsidized owner also walks away with assets of just over $56,000. This represents a 21 percent annual return for the CLT homeowner, given an initial investment of about $15,000 (3 percent down and 3 percent closing costs).

There are good fiscal reasons for limiting the amount of equity a homeowner may remove from a subsidized property at resale. In the case of the homebuyer loan, ensuring the continued affordability of this one home would require a public investment totaling $820,000 over 30 years. If the initial subsidy were instead invested through a CLT, the same house could serve the same number of homebuyers at the same targeted income for the same period of time for a total municipal investment over 30 years of only $50,000.

EFFECTIVE CITY–CLT PARTNERSHIPS

When investing public funds and delegating responsibilities to a nonprofit organization like a CLT, local jurisdictions have legitimate concerns about how their resources will be used and how their partners will perform. Supporting a CLT to expand and preserve a stock of permanently affordable, owner-occupied housing raises crucial questions. How effective will the CLT be in managing this growing inventory of land and housing? Will the CLT's beneficiaries succeed in their venture into homeownership? Will the CLT itself survive?

Based on analysis of selected city–CLT partnerships across the country, it is clear that there are many effective methods and mechanisms to support the projects and operations of a community land trust while also providing prudent municipal oversight of performance. This report presents many

TABLE 1		
Performance of Alternative Subsidies Over Time		
Initial Sale	**Homebuyer Loan (No Interest)**	**CLT Model (AMI Index)**
Initial market value	$250,000	$250,000
Subsidy	50,000	50,000
Initial sale price	250,000	200,000
Resale in Year 7		
Sale price	375,000	245,000
Repay first mortgage	(174,051)	(174,051)
Repay public subsidy	(50,000)	0
Sales costs (6%)	(22,500)	(14,700)
Seller's net proceeds	**128,449**	**56,249**
Affordable price to next buyer	245,000	245,000
Recaptured subsidy	50,000	0
Additional subsidy required	**80,000**	**0**
Total subsidy for next buyer	130,000	0
Resale in Year 14		
Sale price	565,000	303,000
Additional subsidy required	**132,000**	**0**
Resale in Year 21		
Sale price	850,000	372,000
Additional subsidy required	**216,000**	**0**
Resale in Year 28		
Sale price	1,278,000	458,000
Additional subsidy required	**342,000**	**0**
Total subsidy invested over 30 years for 5 families	**$820,000**	**$50,000**

Note: Data assume 6 percent annual home price inflation, 3 percent annual income inflation, and stable interest rates.
Source: Jacobus and Lubell (2007)

options for local government assistance during a CLT's startup, early growth, and mature phases of development, as well as for taxation and regulation of CLT land and homes. Highlighted within each set of options are "model practices" that offer the greatest promise for creating CLTs that are accountable, productive, and sustainable. The report concludes with a discussion of how cities and CLTs are changing the roles they play in their partnership to preserve affordable homeownership.

CHAPTER 2

Supporting CLT Startups

Until recently, most municipalities were willing to commit significant resources to a CLT's projects and operations only *after* the land trust had been established. Today, many jurisdictions either take the lead in creating the CLT or become closely involved soon after neighborhood leaders begin the planning process. Given their early participation and investment in CLT projects, local governments have begun to pay closer attention to the decisions and tasks that lay the foundation for the land trust's success (see box 2).

The critical period in a CLT's startup phase is the year immediately preceding incorporation and the first two years of operation. Local governments can bring a full range of support to the table during this phase, from playing a modest role in publicizing the shared goals of the CLT to making major investments in its portfolio and operations.

Introducing an Unfamiliar Model
In some cities, municipal staff have taken the lead in researching community land trusts and then educating political leaders and the wider community about the model. In Portland, for example, the Bureau of Housing and Community Development originated the idea for a CLT and arranged for CLT practitioners from other cities to participate in local forums for nonprofits and housing activists. In Burlington, members of the city's Community and Economic Development Office organized a series of public information sessions about CLTs. In

The Daniels family enjoys having a yard at their Portland Community Land Trust home in Portland, Oregon.

BOX 2
Building a CLT from the Ground Up: A Startup Checklist

Key Decisions Before Incorporation

- **Beneficiaries.** Who will the CLT serve?

- **Geographic service area.** Where will the CLT operate?

- **Development.** What kinds of housing or other structures will be developed on the CLT's land, and what roles will the CLT play in the development process?

- **Governance.** How will the governing board be structured and selected? Will the CLT have membership? If so, what role(s) will the members play?

- **Resources.** Where will the CLT find funding to pay for projects and operations?

Essential Tasks Before Incorporation

- Assign responsibility for key decisions about CLT structure, service area, beneficiaries, and activities.

- Begin outreach to community residents and key stakeholders.

- Evaluate housing market conditions, optimal prices, and likely demand for units serving the target population.

- Estimate the availability and sufficiency of public and private resources for land acquisition, housing development, housing subsidies, and CLT operations.

- Conduct legal research as needed.

- Prepare documents establishing the CLT and institutionalizing its structure and governance.

Formative Tasks After Incorporation

- Seat and orient the CLT's first board of directors.

- Design the ground lease and resale formula.

- Create an outreach plan and materials for building CLT membership and for educating the broader community.

- Develop and implement homebuyer selection and orientation programs.

- Create a three-year plan for bringing the CLT's portfolio to scale, including a staffing plan, operating budget, policies and procedures, and housing development goals.

- Apply for 501(c)(3) designation as a tax-exempt charitable organization.

- Review municipal and state programs for compatibility with the CLT model and negotiate modifications to expand access to funding sources.

- Negotiate property tax treatment for the CLT's resale-restricted, owner-occupied housing with the local assessor.

- Build relationships with private financial institutions in preparation for mortgaging of CLT housing.

- Develop job descriptions for staff and complete a hiring process.

Chicago, a senior official in the Department of Housing teamed up with a program officer from the MacArthur Foundation to commission a report on the CLT model, and then followed up with individual briefings for foundation staff and various city officials.

Participating in the Planning Process

In many jurisdictions, elected officials and/or municipal staff have taken an active part in planning the CLT. Officials from the Town of Chapel Hill and surrounding Orange County, for example, sat on the advisory committee that created that region's CLT. In Irvine, the mayor and a city council member served on the CLT's planning committee and first board of directors. Irvine's mayor was also the board's first chair. In Chicago, the housing commissioner was part of the advisory committee that created the CLT and now sits on the CLT's board of directors.

MODEL PRACTICE
Early and Ongoing Participation of Community and Municipality

Among the many tasks involved in starting a CLT, none is more important than systematically introducing the model to a wide array of constituencies. The municipal agencies to which the CLT must look for project funding, regulatory approvals, and equitable taxation are a high priority for any campaign of outreach, education, and organizing. It is equally important, however, to reach out to the individuals and institutions that call the CLT's service area their home, as well as to other nonprofit organizations serving the same population. For many of these individuals and groups, these outreach efforts will likely be their first introduction to the CLT model.

Municipalities may resist working with neighborhood activists who are known critics of city hall, or they may simply be reluctant to relinquish control over a fledgling organization that will receive a major commitment of public resources. Particularly if the CLT depends on a municipality's resources and is dominated by its priorities, some of the model's democratic components can be lost. For example, municipal participants may invite nongovernmental constituencies into the process only after critical decisions have been made, or worse, attempt to eliminate community members from the board altogether.

Full participation of both the community and the municipality is essential to create the transparency necessary to make this unconventional model of tenure a success. Including community residents and prospective CLT homebuyers is especially important because they can help the CLT mitigate opposition to its projects, build a market for its homes, and win acceptance among public funders, private lenders, and the community at large.

Staffing the Startup

Municipal employees have sometimes taken responsibility for convening meetings and staffing the CLT's advisory committee and/or governing board. On occasion, they also have assumed primary responsibility for administering the CLT and serving as de facto staff in the early years. For example, the first executive director of the Chicago CLT is a municipal employee working out of the Department of Housing. A city attorney is also providing invaluable legal advice as the CLT's first projects get under way. In Delray Beach, the Community Redevelopment Agency staffs the newly founded CLT.

Contracting for Expert Assistance

Several cities and counties have taken the lead and borne the cost of hiring consultants to assist with planning the CLT. Burlington, Chicago, Delray Beach, Highland Park, Irvine, Phoenix, Portland, San Bernardino County, and Sarasota have contracted with consultants for a wide range of CLT-related services, including advice on organizational development, ground lease issues, project feasibility, and business planning.

Providing Startup Financing

In several cases, municipalities have provided grants to support the planning and incorporation of the CLT. For example, the City Council of Burlington approved a $200,000 startup grant in 1984 for the Burlington Community Land Trust (now the Champlain Housing Trust). In 2003, Hennepin County made a $25,000 grant to fund the research and planning that went into creating the City of Lakes CLT in Minneapolis. In 2006, the Town of Truckee entered into a $45,000 contract for services with the Workforce Housing Association of Truckee–Tahoe to launch a community land trust program.

Retooling Existing Programs

Most cities turn to existing programs and resources to find support for fledgling CLTs. In some cases, this has meant adapting the CLT to existing regulations designed to meet the needs of traditional homeownership subsidy programs. In others, officials have carefully assessed the compatibility of existing housing and community development programs with the CLT model and made modifications where necessary. In Chicago, for example, the housing department made changes in its programs to ensure the new CLT had access to municipal resources. City staff also met with the Cook County tax assessor and secured a commitment to tax CLT homes on the basis of their permanently restricted resale value. Both Portland and Chapel Hill amended their homebuyer assistance programs to allow CLTs to retain public subsidies in CLT homes, requiring no repayment of this municipal investment.

MODEL PRACTICE
Coordination Among Municipal Programs

If two government agencies intend to routinely support a CLT's projects, it makes sense to ensure that their grant and loan agreements, liens, and covenants are consistent with one another. The Community Housing Trust of Sarasota County, for example, worked with the County and City of Sarasota to develop a grant agreement for project development that was acceptable to both. In North Carolina, the Orange Community Housing and Land Trust developed a restrictive covenant that satisfies the administrative needs of both Orange County and the Town of Chapel Hill, allowing the CLT to layer funding from the two sources without regulatory conflicts.

Committing Multiyear Operational Funds

A few municipalities have gone far beyond a one-time startup grant to cover much of a CLT's costs during its first few years of operation. Sarasota County, for example, pledged annual operating grants of $250,000 for the first four years to enable the Community Housing Trust of Sarasota County to build organizational capacity, develop a homeownership program, and launch its first projects. The City of Chicago (with a grant from the MacArthur Foundation) is covering the cost of staffing the new CLT and will pay for overhead and administrative costs during its first few years.

Committing Project Funding and/or Municipal Property

As an inducement for starting a CLT and a means of quickly establishing the CLT's credibility, some municipalities have made an early commitment to building the trust's portfolio. These commitments may come in the form of equity investments or low-interest loans for a CLT's projects, conveyance of publicly owned lands, or conveyance of publicly owned or publicly mandated housing units. In Delray Beach, for example, the Community Redevelopment Agency pledged to convey vacant parcels of land it owned to the CLT. Irvine plans to place most of the inclusionary housing units constructed in future years into the CLT's portfolio. The city's redevelopment agency also intends to donate land and provide funding for the CLT's project developments.

Similarly, community land trusts in Syracuse and Albuquerque were established in part because of the transfer of large parcels of city-owned land for redevelopment. More recently, the city council of Washington, DC, committed $10 million in public funds to help subsidize the first 1,000 units of resale-restricted, owner-occupied housing developed by City First Homes, a District-wide CLT that plans to eventually create 10,000 units of affordable housing.

CHAPTER 3
Building the CLT Portfolio

L ike every nonprofit developer, CLTs face significant challenges in acquiring land and constructing or rehabilitating housing that can be sold at an affordable price to households of modest means. Municipalities have used a variety of strategies to support CLTs during this early growth phase, including donations of publicly owned land and buildings, loans and grants for land acquisition and residential development, dedication of inclusionary housing units, and/or waiver of requirements and fees that add to the cost of housing production.

Donation of Land and Buildings

Municipalities can subsidize a CLT's projects by reaching into their own inventory, either donating land and buildings to the land trust or selling the properties at a discount. These assets may include surplus properties acquired in anticipation of highway extensions or school expansions that never happened, as well as decommissioned airports, firehouses, and other outdated facilities. Municipalities can also convey city-owned residential properties acquired through tax foreclosures or blighted properties purchased for redevelopment.

For example, the City of Syracuse deeded 12.5 acres of vacant land to Jubilee Homes, a nonprofit developer jointly controlled by the city and the Time of Jubilee CLT. When each single-family house constructed on the site was sold, the underlying land was conveyed to the CLT. The Delray Beach Community Redevelopment Authority conveyed parcels of land at

The Manabos
are new members
of the Kulshan
Community Land
Trust in Bellingham,
Washington.

Dudley Village was developed by Dorchester Bay Economic Development Corporation to provide 50 affordable housing units for the Dudley Neighbors, Inc. community land trust in the Roxbury neighborhood of Boston, Massachusetts.

a discounted price to the Delray Beach CLT for infill housing. The Cuyahoga CLT built homes on tax-foreclosed parcels of land conveyed by the City of Cleveland. Multnomah County conveyed tax-foreclosed lands to the Portland CLT, on which the PCLT has constructed limited-equity homes.

Burlington donated a decommissioned firehouse to the Champlain Housing Trust for conversion into temporary housing for homeless families. Boston donated roughly 30 acres of blighted and abandoned property to Dudley Neighbors, Inc., a CLT affiliated with the Dudley Street Neighborhood Initiative. This donation helped DNI develop 155 units of affordable housing, rehabilitate a commercial building, and add open space to the community.

Loans and Grants

Many municipalities provide direct cash subsidies to CLTs to lower the price of their single-family houses or condominiums. Subsidies may be structured as grants or as deferred-payment, forgivable loans. Most development loans from local governments function exactly like grants in that they are interest-free, require no monthly payments, and are forgiven if the CLT successfully completes and monitors the project for a specified period. Loans may give a municipality more options for enforcement if the CLT fails to perform as agreed. The tradeoff for this added security is that loans can complicate homebuyer financing and require significantly more upfront legal work for both the CLT and the municipality.

Minneapolis, for example, provides interest-free, deferred loans with a 30-year term to the City of Lakes CLT. The loans are forgiven at maturity as long as the CLT consistently meets the city's performance standards. Many other CLTs—including those in Albuquerque, Burlington, Highland Park, Lawrence, Orange County, Portland, Sarasota County, and Washington,

DC—have also received grants or no-interest loans from local jurisdictions. The most common sources of CLT project grants are pass-through HOME and CDBG funds, along with municipal revenues administered by local housing trust funds. In one case, Burlington, the municipality loaned employee pension funds to a local CLT for the development of resale-restricted homes.

Inclusionary Housing

A growing number of municipalities strongly encourage, if not require, the inclusion of affordable units in market-rate developments (see box 3). Private developers are often eager to find a means of meeting these long-term affordability requirements without having to monitor and report on the inclusionary units they build. A CLT is perfectly positioned to be the long-term steward for these housing resources, given that it already fulfills these responsibilities for other resale-restricted units in its portfolio. CLT oversight is also in the jurisdiction's best interest because many for-profit development companies dissolve after they complete their projects.

In most cases, developers build the inclusionary units and then turn the homes over to the CLT. Petaluma, for example, has encouraged developers of several subdivisions to meet its city-mandated inclusionary requirements by conveying homes to the Housing Land Trust of Sonoma County. Under these agreements, developers sell the homes to CLT-selected buyers and simultaneously donate the land under the homes to the land trust. In Burlington, the Champlain Housing Trust (CHT) manages over 100 owner-occupied condominiums built under the city's inclusionary zoning ordinance. Because the units are in mixed-income

---

BOX 3
A Town-Brokered Partnership for Inclusionary Housing

When the Centex Corporation, one of the country's largest private home builders, proposed a 200-unit townhouse development in Chapel Hill, the town strongly requested that the proposed project have an affordable component and encouraged Centex to work with the Orange Community Housing and Land Trust (OCHLT) to preserve the affordability of the homes. Centex agreed to sell 30 units to OCHLT at a below-market price.

For its part, OCHLT agreed to market the units during the construction period and to buy them from Centex after qualified buyers had obtained financing. The developer paid a $2,500–3,000 fee to OCHLT for marketing and selling the affordable units. The project's market-rate units were sized at approximately 2,000 square feet, with prices ranging from $230,000 to $275,000. OCHLT worked closely with Centex to design somewhat smaller but similarly high-quality units that OCHLT could sell for $90,000 to $105,000. This involved considerable negotiation around both the mix and pricing of units, with compromises reached on both issues.

Partnerships between private developers and CLTs have proven to be a workable and effective strategy for creating affordable housing. OCHLT Executive Director Robert Dowling is quick to point out, however, that the partnership between Centex and OCHLT would never have happened without the town's involvement.

The City's Edge Condominiums were developed by the Champlain Housing Trust as part of a larger mixed-use development in Burlington, Vermont.

buildings, the developers do not transfer land to the trust, but instead record covenants against the unit deeds that allow CHT to repurchase the condos at affordable prices when owners move.

Regulatory Concessions

Municipalities sometimes support development of CLT homes by reducing or waiving application and impact fees, relaxing zoning requirements for parking or lot coverage, and offering other regulatory concessions. Since this regulatory relief increases the project's profitability, it is another form of local government subsidy to the housing developer. The public value created through this relief should therefore be preserved over time, just as cash subsidies are.

Some jurisdictions provide relief and incentives only to developers that promise long-term or permanent affordability of the units. Burlington, for example, reduces or waives impact fees for newly constructed homes with lasting affordability controls. The more affordable the home and the longer the period of affordability, the greater is the reduction in fees. The City of Bellingham offers a 50-percent density bonus to developers who agree to keep all units permanently affordable to income-qualified buyers. The city may also adjust zoning requirements for minimum lot size, street frontage, setbacks, parking, and usable open space.

CHAPTER 4
Sustaining CLT Operations

As a CLT undertakes projects and builds a portfolio of resale-restricted units, it can begin to generate an increasing share of its operating revenues from development fees, marketing fees, lease fees, and other project-related income. And once the CLT has established a track record, it can often attract foundation funding, corporate grants, and individual donations. A number of older CLTs have in fact reached a scale in their holdings and operations—a "sustainability threshold"—where they generate sufficient income to cover the cost of their stewardship responsibilities. It is important to note, however, that even mature CLTs may continue to depend on external support from local governments or private foundations. Once a CLT's portfolio grows to a certain size, though, this support can be directed toward new programs or projects rather than toward the stewardship of existing affordable housing.

In contrast to project development subsidies, external support for CLT operations is used for general organizational and administrative expenses such as staff salaries, office rent, supplies, and program costs not directly related to a specific housing development. While the mix varies greatly state by state, city by city, and even CLT by CLT, the most common sources of operating support are local government funds, private contributions, and revenues from development projects.

Grants from Local Government
Many local governments provide general operating grants to CLTs, while others provide support for specific programs such as home-buyer outreach and education. Funds may come from a variety of sources.

- *Community Development Block Grants.* CLTs often receive operating grants out of a local government's allocation of federal CDBG funds. The City of Albuquerque, for example, provides Sawmill CLT with annual grants of $200,000 from CDBG monies that can be used for staff salaries, predevelopment work, and building organizational capacity.

North Missoula Community Development Corporation used HOME and TIF funds to build Clark Fork Commons in Missoula, Montana.

- *HOME capacity grants.* Many CLTs are designated as Community Housing Development Organizations (CHDOs) and receive capacity grants out a local government's annual allocation from the federal HOME Investment Partnership Program. CHDO operating grants are a common source of support for CLTs across the country. Homestead CLT in Seattle, for example, receives $30,000 in CHDO funding from the King County HOME program.

- *Local housing trust funds.* In some cases, municipalities use housing trust fund revenues to support actual projects and to build the capacity of nonprofit housing developers such as CLTs. The City of Highland Park, for example, provides annual grants of $100,000 from its Affordable Housing Trust Fund to support operations of the Highland Park CLT. The housing trust fund in Burlington, which is capitalized through a 1-percent add-on to the city's property tax rate, distributes annual "capacity grants" that may be used to support the staffing, training, planning, fundraising, or ongoing operations of nonprofit corporations that develop permanently affordable housing.

- *Other municipal sources.* City or county general funds, housing bond proceeds, and tax increment financing (TIF) revenues may provide additional support for CLT operations. For example, the Delray Beach Community Redevelopment Agency has committed a portion of its TIF revenues to cover the annual operating expenses of the Delray Beach CLT.

MODEL PRACTICE
Multiyear Funding Commitments

With a commitment for a particular level of external support, a CLT can be more aggressive in its growth plans, develop new programs more quickly, and offer more stable jobs (thereby attracting more qualified staff). Predictable multiyear funding can also help a CLT secure other public and private revenues, leveraging the municipality's investment many times over.

Under this arrangement, municipal officials and CLT staff should meet each year to discuss progress, identify mutual goals for the coming year, and set the amount of the grant renewal. If the CLT is not performing as promised or if sufficient funds are not available, the municipality can reduce the amount of the grant. Similarly, if the CLT exceeds expectations or makes a convincing case for more funding, the municipality can increase the grant beyond the initial commitment. The City of Albuquerque's five-year plan, for example, provides CDBG funds to the Sawmill CLT for operating support. The city initially allocated $150,000 per year to the CLT, but increased the amount to $200,000 in 2007 because of both the CLT's project success and its operational needs.

Donations from Private Sources

As a 510(c)(3) charitable organization, a CLT can generally leverage public sector investment with private tax-deductible contributions. In a national survey of CLTs conducted by the Lincoln Institute in 2006, half of the 119 respondents reported receiving private donations (Sungu-Eryilmaz and Greenstein 2007). A smaller unpublished survey conducted the same year by Jeff Corey of the Northern Communities CLT in Duluth and Jeff Washburne of the City of Lakes CLT in Minneapolis found that CLTs received between 10 percent and 70 percent of their operating revenue from private sources such as the following.

- *Foundation grants.* Community foundations, family foundations, and larger grant-making foundations with an interest in affordable housing are frequent CLT contributors. While a few provide ongoing, unrestricted operating funds, foundations usually tie their grants to specific outcomes or programs. The California Community Foundation, for example, recognized how rapidly rising land costs were eroding its ability to support affordable housing in the Los Angeles region and founded the Community Foundation Land Trust. Its contribution of $3.8 million can be used for operations and initial projects.

- *Corporate contributions.* Corporate donors tend to fall into one of three categories: housing industry players, including banks, mortgage lenders, and secondary market institutions; large local employers with an interest in expanding the supply of workforce housing; and other civic leaders who support the CLT in exchange for high-profile recognition.

- *Individual donations.* Some CLTs direct ongoing fundraising efforts at the local community. Although time-consuming, these programs can generate significant revenue and build important community goodwill. In fact, some small CLTs, such as the Community Land Trust Association of West Marin (CLAM) in Point Reyes Station, raise the majority of their annual operating budgets from individual donations. Among the CLTs consulted for this report, however, local fundraising accounted for an average of only 5 percent of operating revenue.

Revenues from Project Development
The majority of CLTs collect fees for each unit of affordable housing they help to develop. Development fees may be structured as a flat amount per unit or as a percentage of total development costs. The City of Madison, for example, allows the Madison Area CLT to take a developer fee of up to 15 percent of a project's total costs.

CLTs that are not directly involved in housing development often provide comprehensive marketing services that include everything from outreach to potential homebuyers to working with local lenders to help applicants qualify for mortgages. Some charge a per-unit fee for these services that typically amounts to no more than 3 percent of the sales price. Other CLTs collect a flat fee for every home sold. The City of Lakes CLT in Minneapolis, for example, charges a marketing fee of $2,500 per unit regardless of the selling price.

Revenues from Ongoing Operations
CLTs also generate operating income from a number of internal sources, which steadily increase as their portfolios of land and housing grow larger.

- *Ground lease fees.* A CLT's ground lease fees are its most reliable revenue source. While a few CLTs now charge as much as $100 per month, these fees tend to be in the $25–50 range, set well below the market value of the leasehold to keep the homes affordable. Even at this low price, however, CLTs with multiple properties in their portfolios can realize significant revenues from this source. Thistle Community Housing in Boulder, for example, reports that ground lease fees averaging $30 a month on its 211 resale-restricted, owner-occupied units cover almost a third of the cost of running its CLT program.

- *Lease reissuance/resale fees.* An increasing number of CLTs collect fees when units change hands, using these revenues to defray some of the costs of managing the transfer. In some cases, the fee is charged to the sellers, reducing their proceeds in the same way a broker's commission would. In other cases, the fee is added to the resale price, increasing the cost of the home to the next buyer. OPAL CLT on Orcus Island, for example, charges a 1-percent fee to both the buyers and sellers of a home, netting the CLT a 2-percent fee on each resale.

- *Membership dues.* Area residents who support the CLT generally pay annual membership dues ranging from $1 to $50. Although membership income is a small factor in most CLT budgets, it can provide a predictable source of revenue that grows steadily as an organization matures. With more than 4,000 members, the Champlain Housing Trust in Burlington collects over $70,000 in membership fees annually, covering about 5 percent of its operating budget.

OPAL Community Land Trust built these two new homes on donated land near the village center of Eastsound, Orcus Island, Washington.

- *Fee-for-service income.* Some CLTs earn fees for performing specific services such as educating prospective homebuyers, packaging loans for local mortgage lenders, and monitoring local inclusionary housing units on behalf of a city or county.

CHAPTER 5
Taxing CLT Property

Given that the price of CLT homes is determined by formula and not by the market, local tax assessments can significantly affect the afford-ability of CLT homes (see box 4). If property taxes are high at the time of purchase, CLTs may need to either increase the subsidy to homebuyers or serve homebuyers with higher incomes. If property taxes rise during their tenure, owners have less of their limited income available to cover other household expenses, including maintenance. As a result, CLT homes can become steadily less affordable and less sustainable.

State judicial, legislative, and administrative guidelines regulate the taxation of CLT prop-erties, although local assessors often retain wide discretion in interpreting and applying these guidelines. Few standardized policies and procedures exist for valuing and taxing CLT homes, however, resulting in great variation from one jurisdiction to another, both across and within states.

Given that a municipality and a CLT have a common interest in the continuing afford-ability of resale-restricted, owner-occupied housing, they also have a common interest in equitable taxation. Nevertheless, owners of CLT homes often pay more than their fair share of local property taxes because assessors do not take into account the durable restric-tions that significantly reduce the property's marketability and profitability. Similarly, assessors often overlook the fact that CLT land is leased out for 99 years for monthly fees that are typically far below the market rate of the leasehold.

BOX 4
Impact of Property Taxes on Affordability

Consider the case where a CLT has received enough grant support from a municipality to remove from its sale price the entire cost of the underlying land and a portion of the cost of construction. This enables the CLT to sell a house having a market value of $210,000 for the relatively affordable price of $85,000. If the CLT restricts the resale price of this house, using a formula that allows the homeowner to pocket 25 percent of the appreciated market value when the property is resold, the maximum price of the unit will be $116,804 after seven years of occupancy (assuming market appreciation of 7 percent annually).

	Market Value of the CLT House	Restricted Resale Price of the CLT House
Initial Purchase	$210,000	$85,000
End of Year 1	$224,700	$88,675
End of Year 2	$240,429	$92,607
End of Year 3	$257,259	$96,815
End of Year 4	$275,267	$101,317
End of Year 5	$294,536	$106,134
End of Year 6	$315,154	$111,288
End of Year 7	$337,215	$116,804

The home's market value, however, will have reached $337,215 by the end of Year 7. If the municipal assessment does not take account of either the initial below-market purchase price or the permanently restricted resale price, the owner of this CLT house will be forced to pay property taxes not only on the $116,804 of value to which she has title, but also on $220,411 of value that she does not own and can never claim. A house that was *made* more affordable by the municipality's subsidy and *kept* more affordable by the CLT's resale restrictions is therefore made less and less affordable by the municipality's taxation policy.

Tax policy can thus be an enormous barrier to the expansion of resale-restricted housing, especially where the market value of residential real estate is rising rapidly and property taxes are keeping pace. At a certain point, no matter how affordable the purchase price of a CLT home may once have been, taxes that are pegged to a property's market value rather than to its restricted resale price will eventually render the cost of holding the home unaffordable for households of modest means.

To preserve the affordability of their units, many CLTs have successfully persuaded local assessors to value and tax CLT homes differently than market-rate homes. Equitable taxation of CLT property relates to three basic issues: (1) the value of a resale-restricted CLT home when first entered on the local tax rolls; (2) the value of land owned by the CLT when first entered on the tax rolls; and (3) the revaluation of a CLT home over time.

Valuation of CLT Homes

A growing number of state and municipal officials now recognize that taxing resale-restricted homes at their market value is contrary to the community's interest in creating and maintaining affordable homeownership opportunities. Even among these jurisdictions, though, the calculation of assessments varies widely. In Boulder County and Los Angeles County, the assessed value of CLT homes when entered on the tax rolls is the (heavily subsidized) purchase price that lower-income households pay. In Orange County, North Carolina, in contrast, the assessor typically values CLT properties at about $10,000 more than the initial purchase price, but provides no specific formula for the calculation. In Burlington, the assessed value of the owner-occupied homes in the Champlain Housing Trust's portfolio is set at 37 percent below the market value of a similar property.

MODEL PRACTICE
Fair Taxation of CLT Homes

The assessed value of any buildings located on CLT land should reflect the permanent restrictions that the ground lease imposes on their use and resale. Assessed values should therefore be lower than those of similar but unencumbered buildings. Given that a buyer would not reasonably pay more than the CLT's formula price for a restricted unit, this price is generally the best indicator of the "fair value" of a CLT home.

When levying taxes on properties developed by the Highland Park CLT, for example, Moraine Township recognizes that the resale restrictions significantly reduce the market value of CLT lands and homes. The township's official assessment policy notes that affordable properties with resale control mechanisms are not comparable to market-rate properties because of these restrictions. CLT properties are therefore assessed at a level that reflects their resale-restricted value, which is much lower than their market value. It is the established policy of the Moraine Township that assessments of CLT homes are based upon the net sales price to the buyers.

The Temple townhouses were the first new condominium project of the Highland Park Illinois Community Land Trust.

Valuation of CLT Land

Apart from the homes themselves, there is a question of how land owned by the CLT should be valued and taxed. Most CLTs enter into long-term ground leases that severely limit their ability to change the use of the land or to collect significant income from it. In addition, most CLTs charge only a nominal fee for using their land, a fee that is pegged to the affordability of the homes rather than to the appraised value of the land. Indeed, in most housing markets, the CLT's ground lease fee is set far below what a market rent would be. This is a conscious decision, motivated by the CLT's charitable mission to help lower-income people become homeowners.

Taking into account the enduring use of the leased land and the below-market revenues it generates, many jurisdictions assess CLT land considerably below market value. In Delray Beach, for example, the assessor has determined that the land beneath the resale-restricted homes of the Delray Beach CLT has no value at all because it has been turned over indefinitely to CLT homeowners for a nominal lease fee. More commonly, assessors see the land as having some (although greatly reduced) residual value. A typical approach is to value CLT land based on the stream of income that it produces from the lease fees paid by the homeowners who reside on the land.

Revaluation of CLT Homes over Time

If assessments of CLT homes are based on the initially affordable sales prices, but then are allowed to increase at the same rate as prices for market-rate properties, CLT homeowners will eventually have to pay taxes on values far above the restricted resale prices. Given that the resale price of a CLT home will nearly always rise more slowly than the resale price of a comparable market-rate home, many local assessors peg their periodic reassessments of CLT property to the maximum price contractually permitted by the CLT's resale formula.

Winner of the 2007 AARP and NAHB Livable Communities Award, the mixed-income housing at Troy Gardens developed by the Madison (Wisconsin) Area Community Land Trust is green-built, fully accessible, and clustered to preserve open space.

This 3-bedroom, active solar modular duplex, located in Lafayette, Colorado, is a property of Thistle Community Housing.

MODEL PRACTICE
Fair Taxation of Increased Home Values

Post-purchase adjustments to the assessments of CLT homes should take the CLT's long-term price controls into account. Ideally, assessors should base the maximum price of a CLT home on the resale formula in the ground lease and then adjust the assessed value accordingly. Boulder County taxes the homes of its local CLT, Thistle Community Housing, according to the current price that each unit would realize if sold under the terms of the ground lease. Each year, Thistle recalculates the resale prices for the homes in its portfolio and submits the figures to the county assessor. Dudley Neighbors, Inc., has negotiated a similar arrangement with the tax assessor in Boston.

The assessor in Madison uses a variant of this approach. The Madison Area CLT allows its homeowners to keep 25 percent of the home's appreciation upon resale. The city assessor enters the homes on the tax rolls at their original purchase prices and then adjusts the prices annually at a rate equal to 25 percent of the appreciation of comparable market-rate homes.

When municipalities delegate responsibility for the stewardship of resale-restricted, owner-occupied housing to a CLT, they must still "watch the watcher." Under normal conditions, local government can take a hands-off approach, leaving the routine tasks of monitoring and enforcing use and resale restrictions to the CLT. In extreme cases, however, the municipality may need to remind the CLT of its contractual obligations or even take legal action to compel the CLT to perform as promised. Municipalities typically attempt to protect themselves against three types of performance failure.

- ***Failure to protect the occupancy and condition of assisted homes.*** The municipality depends on the CLT to monitor and enforce the terms of the ground lease so that assisted homes remain owner-occupied and in good repair. These requirements include ensuring that CLT homeowners pay their taxes, comply with local zoning and building codes, and carry insurance on their homes.

- ***Failure to preserve the affordability of assisted homes.*** The CLT is also responsible for ensuring that homes are sold only to income-eligible buyers for the formula-determined price. Allowing municipally assisted homes to sell for more than the formula price or to be bought by households earning more than the eligibility standard usually violates the terms of the CLT's grant or loan agreement with the municipality.

- ***Dissolution of the CLT.*** Failure of a CLT should not jeopardize either the security of leaseholders or the affordability of their subsidized homes. Under the terms of virtually all CLT ground leases, the sale or transfer of a CLT's land (whether voluntary or involuntary) does not disturb the lease. Some municipal sponsors require a dissolving CLT to transfer its land to another nonprofit with an affordable housing mission or to the municipality itself.

Municipal Performance Requirements

When a local government gives project or operating support to a CLT, the grant or loan agreement ordinarily specifies the CLT's responsibilities. Every municipality has its own list of performance requirements, which can be short or long, general or specific, flexible or rigid. The CLT activities most commonly subject to municipal oversight include the following.

- ***Developing CLT homes***. The municipality may require the CLT to perform such development-related tasks as coordinating site acquisition, securing planning approvals and building permits, participating in project design, obtaining financing, and overseeing construction of new units.

- ***Marketing CLT homes.*** Cities, counties, and towns that invest in a CLT's homeownership projects often require the CLT to market the homes in an open and transparent way, in compliance with federal, state, and local fair housing laws. This is to ensure that all income-eligible citizens have an equal chance to learn about and apply for these publicly assisted homes.

Durham Community Land Trustees in Durham, North Carolina, is expanding its portfolio to include rental and green units, like these passive solar apartments in the Brite Horizon development.

- *Selecting prospective homebuyers.* While most municipalities rely on CLTs to choose the households that will have an opportunity to purchase homes, some require the CLT to submit the selection criteria for approval before marketing begins. Most local governments rely on the CLT to verify that applicants meet the selection criteria, although some require documentation of eligibility either before closing or later as part of an annual report.

- *Initial pricing of CLT homes.* Most municipalities allow the CLT to set initial prices consistent with local guidelines. Some cities, such as Bellingham, review every transaction before closing to ensure that homes are sold at an affordable price. Other cities, such as Madison, set their own maximum prices for affordable ownership units.

MODEL PRACTICE
Adequate Spread Between Home Prices and Income Eligibility Criteria

A necessary and important distinction must be made between the percentage of area median income (AMI) used to set the price of a CLT home and the percentage of AMI used to determine the eligibility of a homebuyer. For example, homes that must be sold to buyers earning no more than 80 percent of AMI might be priced to be affordable to a household earning 70 percent of AMI. Setting these maximums with a 10-percent spread increases the pool of prospective homebuyers.

- *Monitoring and enforcing homeowner compliance.* Ideally municipal officials choose to regulate CLT homeowners indirectly through the CLT ground lease. The ground lease contains restrictions to ensure the homes are used in ways that conform to the goals of the municipality's affordable homeownership program. The CLT is required by the municipality to monitor compliance with the lease and report any violations.

- *Maintaining affordability.* A CLT's resale formula is clearly spelled out in the ground lease and, in some cases, repeated in the municipality's loan or grant agreements. Occasionally, municipal officials become involved in designing or amending the resale formula for consistency with existing housing programs or goals. Most municipalities are not, however, involved in the transfer of individual homes, relying instead on the CLT to ensure they sell at affordable prices.

MODEL PRACTICE
Backup Notice to the Municipality

Under the terms of the model CLT ground lease, homeowners must notify the CLT whenever they decide to sell. The lease also gives the CLT a time-limited option to purchase the home at the formula price. Some municipalities, fearing the CLT might fail to act during this critical period, have suggested that CLT homeowners notify the municipality as well as the CLT. Taking a blended approach, the City of Santa Monica requires owners of CLT homes to notify the city of their intent to sell and to offer the city an option to purchase their homes at the formula price—but only if the CLT fails to respond to the homeowner's first notice.

- *Maintaining CLT homes.* For affordable homes to meet the needs of future generations, the units must be maintained properly and upgraded periodically. CLTs can encourage good practices by educating homebuyers about maintenance; monitoring and enforcing the maintenance provisions of the lease; arranging for home maintenance financing for CLT homeowners; and, in some cases, coordinating repairs at the time of unit transfers.

MODEL PRACTICE
Regulating the CLT, Not the Homeowner

Some municipalities record covenants or deed restrictions against CLT homes, supplementing provisions in the regulatory agreements already executed with the CLT. Homeowners are then regulated by both the CLT's ground lease and the municipality's covenant. At best, these double documents contain similar provisions. At worst, they contain requirements that are confusing or contradictory.

Municipalities can protect the public's interest in CLT homes by including all of the provisions for assisted housing in the ground lease alone. Setting up this arrangement can involve considerable time, however, because the municipality must first identify all requirements imposed by its ordinances, regulations, and funding sources and then work with the CLT to ensure that the ground lease contains the appropriate language. Over the long term this framework is far easier to understand and administer because the municipality regulates the performance of only one entity, the CLT. This approach also has the advantage of simplifying resales, since the ground lease is the only document that needs to be amended.

Legal Agreements for Protecting Municipal Interests

Loan agreements, grant agreements, or covenants used by local governments typically require the CLT to monitor leases, enforce occupancy restrictions, and protect the affordability of CLT homes in the event of resale, refinancing, default, or foreclosure. Sometimes these agreements include contingencies in the event of the CLT's failure to perform these essential tasks. Municipalities may also use these agreements, along with other mechanisms, to prevent the sale of a CLT's land or to deal with the dissolution of the corporation. The instruments that municipalities most commonly use to regulate CLTs are:

- grants with no remedy for failure to perform;
- grants requiring repayment of funds in the event of default;
- grants secured with covenants or deed restrictions;
- loans secured by liens on CLT land; or
- purchase options that allow the municipality to buy CLT land in the event of default.

The Bell family owns a home in partnership with the Kulshan Community Land Trust in Bellingham, Washington.

Regardless of the approach used, the legal documents typically include the following provisions to protect the municipality's interests without jeopardizing either the homeowners' access to mortgage financing or their security of tenure.

- *Performance standards.* To be effective enforcement tools, loan documents must be clear about what the CLT is supposed to do. The CLT's obligations might include complying with fair housing laws, conducting an open marketing process, monitoring owner occupancy, and enforcing provisions of the CLT lease.

- *Events of default.* The loan documents should spell out the circumstances that constitute a CLT's default. These might include failure to meet any of the municipality's performance standards, as well as any attempt by the CLT to sell its land or to dissolve its corporation.

- *Opportunity to cure.* The loan documents should outline a process through which the CLT receives notice from the municipality of any default and has an opportunity to cure the problem before the local government takes further action.

- *Remedies.* In the rare situation where a problem goes unresolved, the regulatory documents should outline the jurisdiction's possible remedies. While repayment of loan funds may be an appropriate option in some situations, jurisdictions should have other choices, including the right to ask a court to require the CLT to perform specific actions in enforcing its own ground lease and in meeting its contractual obligations to the municipality.

- *Nondisturbance of the ground lease.* The regulatory documents should clearly state that, if the municipality takes possession of the land, the CLT ground lease will survive the transfer and the municipality will recognize the rights of the homeowners and their lenders.

None of these provisions has proven to be a barrier to obtaining private financing for CLT homes. The practice that has sometimes caused problems, though, is structuring a subsidy in the form of a loan secured by a government lien on the CLT's land. Liens create complications for homebuyers and add very little security for the municipality. In addition, loans recorded against the CLT's land must be treated as liabilities on the CLT's balance sheet. Moreover, the land securing the loans is generally booked at a greatly reduced value because of the CLT's long-term lease, further damaging the CLT's financial position.

MODEL PRACTICE
Grants Secured by Covenants

Many CLTs and their municipal partners have concluded that grant agreements, supplemented with covenants or deed restrictions, provide the best way to protect the municipality's interests. A number of municipalities have used these mechanisms to provide a range of options for curing a CLT's failures.

Orange County, North Carolina, for example, provided housing bond funds and HOME funds to the Orange Community Housing and Land Trust for a 32-unit development in Chapel Hill. Orange County and OCHLT executed both a development agreement stating the CLT's project development responsibilities and a grant agreement detailing its long-term obligations in maintaining the occupancy and affordability of the units. The county then required OCHLT to record a declaration of restrictive covenants that secures performance of the requirements contained in the other two documents; requires OCHLT to preserve affordability of the units through a 99-year ground lease; and declares both the county and the Town of Chapel Hill to be "third party beneficiaries of and successors to each and every remedy intended to assure the long-term affordability of the housing."

CHAPTER 7
Trends in City– CLT Partnerships

O ver the past decade, the relationship between municipalities and community land trusts has shifted from adversarial to collaborative as the two have joined in partnerships to achieve their common goals. In the years ahead, their working relationship may evolve even more significantly as cities play a more dominant role in the startup and operation of CLTs, and as CLTs become more focused on stewardship than on development. While holding special promise for bringing CLTs to scale, these trends challenge the ways in which the model has been structured, championed, and applied for most of its history (see box 5).

FROM CITY-AS-SUPPORTER TO CITY-AS-INSTIGATOR

In the past, the initiative for organizing a CLT nearly always came from individuals or organizations outside of local government. If municipal officials participated at all, they were drawn into the process after local community members had made most of the key organizational decisions for setting up the CLT.

Today, a municipality is just as likely to be the driving force behind a CLT as it is to be an impartial lender or grantmaker. Municipal officials in Highland Park, Irvine, and Chicago, for example, took the lead in evaluating the feasibility of a new CLT, introducing this unfamiliar model to the public and providing staff to plan and organize the startup process.

Municipal leadership clearly brings several advantages to the new organization. In particular, local government sponsorship often provides direct access to both federal and local subsidies to acquire land and build housing. Municipal employees may staff the new CLT, further speeding development of the CLT's first projects. Moreover, municipal sponsorship often results in the CLT becoming a favored beneficiary of inclusionary zoning, density bonuses, or other regulatory measures that require private developers to provide affordable units.

CLTs formed by local government face a special set of challenges, however. Winning popular acceptance for a new CLT may be difficult when a municipal sponsor has neither the staff to run a participatory planning process nor the street-level credibility to attract grassroots leaders. Especially in neighborhoods scarred by urban renewal or municipal neglect, residents may regard a CLT started by local government with suspicion and leave the program with little support in the larger community.

Municipally sponsored CLTs also tend to focus only on housing, ignoring the model's potential for holding lands, developing projects, and mobilizing constituencies for nonresidential activities. Particularly when a local government starts a CLT expressly to enhance the effectiveness and longevity of its affordable housing investments, it is unlikely to take a more comprehensive approach to community development and community empowerment.

Major Trends in Affordable Housing Policy and City–CLT Partnerships, 1980–2008

Federal Housing Policy	State and Local Housing Policy	City–CLT Partnerships
• Reduction in federal funding for affordable housing and community development.	• Creation of state and local housing trust funds, capitalized through nonfederal funding sources.	• Expanded number of CLTs working in partnership with local government instead of in opposition to municipal policies and plans.
• Devolution of authority and responsibility for housing and community development programs from the federal government to state and local governments.	• Expanded use of regulatory mandates such as inclusionary zoning and growth management controls that require developers to produce affordable housing.	• Expanded number of cities playing a lead role in starting CLTs instead of waiting for new CLTs to emerge from the community.
• Expanded use of tax credits instead of grants in subsidizing production of affordable housing.	• Expanded use of regulatory incentives such as streamlining, density bonuses, and fee waivers that reward developers for producing affordable housing.	• Expanded number of cities playing a more dominant role in governing CLTs.
• Expansion of capacity funding and technical assistance for Community Housing Development Organizations (including CLTs).	• Wider commitment to preserving the affordability of owner-occupied housing created through the investment of public funds or the exercise of public powers.	• Expanded number of CLTs focusing on stewardship, acting on a city's behalf to monitor and enforce long-term controls over affordability.

FROM CITY-AS-PARTICIPANT TO CITY-AS-GOVERNOR

A more serious challenge for municipally sponsored CLTs is getting government to let go. Having controlled the startup process, some in city hall may want to remain involved by governing the organization as well.

From the earliest days of the CLT movement, most land trusts included at least one local government employee or elected official within the one-third of board members designated as public representatives. These officials were usually nominated and appointed by the rest of the CLT's directors, who were themselves elected by CLT members. Municipal representatives were seldom appointed by a mayor or city council, and were not authorized to speak on the municipality's behalf. Their role was simply to serve as an informal conduit for the flow of information between the CLT and the city.

In recent years, the number of seats reserved for municipal representatives has increased and the power to decide who fills the seats has passed to municipal authorities outside of the CLT. In a growing number of CLTs, all of the public representatives on the board are both affiliated with and appointed by a local government. Even so, more public representative seats on a CLT's board does not necessarily translate into municipal control, especially if the seats are split among several municipalities or among multiple departments within the same municipality. In the cases of the Champlain Housing Trust and the Orange Community Housing and Land Trust, for example, municipal officials occupy a third of the seats on the governing boards, but the representatives come from four different towns in those regions.

In a few recent cases, however, the municipality plays a more dominant role. The City of Irvine, for instance, appointed every member of the initial board of the Irvine Community Land Trust and has retained the right to appoint a third of the seats on all future boards. The Chicago CLT, an initiative of the City of Chicago, has a classic three-part governing board, but the mayor and city council appoint every member. As an even more extreme example of municipal control, the City of Flagstaff operates a CLT as an internal program with no separate identity from local government.

In some places, greater municipal involvement in governance may be a practical and productive strategy, either as a temporary arrangement until the CLT is firmly established or as a permanent alternative to the classic community-based structure. However, the consensus among most practitioners who staff, assist, or fund CLTs is that community land trusts are more successful when they are structured and perceived as somewhat independent of their municipal sponsors. Too close an affiliation with local government may create trouble for the CLT in marketing its homes, diversifying its funding, and retaining its community base.

How much separation a CLT should have from its supporting municipality and how accountable a CLT should be to local residents relative to local government are open questions. The classic CLT provides a very specific organizational recipe: (1) a corporate membership open to any adult resident of the CLT's service area; (2) a governing board composed of equal numbers of lessees, corporate members who are not lessees, and any other category of persons described in the CLT's bylaws; and (3) direct election of a majority of the board by the CLT's members. This structure reflects both the federal definition of a community land trust adopted by Congress in 1992 and the definition of the classic CLT model approved by the National CLT Network in 2006.

Many of today's CLTs do not match this definition. Recognizing this reality, the National CLT Network has opened its membership to land trusts that are variants of the classic model. For example, an organization is eligible to join the network even if it lacks a voting membership, "as long as some structure exists to ensure the board's accountability to the residents of its service area." In addition, there is no barrier to membership in the National CLT Network if the CLT is sponsored by local government—even if more than a third of the seats are taken by municipal appointees or employees.

This signals a shift in the company that older CLTs have been willing to keep, as well as a major change in what it means to be a CLT. Is there some point between being completely independent of and completely controlled by local government where a CLT can no longer be considered a *community* land trust? More practically, is there some point where the ability to succeed as a CLT is undermined by too tight a municipal rein over its assets and operations, or too dominant a municipal presence on the CLT's board? These are questions that the CLT Network, CLT practitioners, and municipal officials will wrestle with for years to come.

FROM CLT-AS-DEVELOPER TO CLT-AS-STEWARD

Most CLTs play the role and perform the tasks of a real estate developer, using their own employees to initiate, manage, and market newly constructed or rehabilitated housing. Some CLTs have spearheaded nonresidential projects as well, including development of commercial buildings, nonprofit incubators, and community centers.

Development is not the CLT's forté, however. Nothing in the model's distinctive approach to ownership, organization, and operation makes real estate development easier or cheaper to do. Indeed, nothing makes a CLT a better developer than any other nonprofit or for-profit entity that has municipal support to produce affordable housing or other community facilities. Instead, the model's real strength lies in protecting a municipality's investment and a community's assets, and in preserving access to land and housing for people of modest means. It is in the period after a project is developed that a CLT makes its most durable and distinctive contribution to a community's well-being (see box 6).

This is not to say that CLTs have wrongly become developers. The organizers of local CLTs eagerly and reasonably took on the developer's role when offered, for example, a once-in-a-lifetime chance to develop a sizable parcel of city-owned land (as in Albuquerque); or priority access to municipal or state funding for the construction of affordable housing (as in Burlington); or millions of dollars from local employers to build starter homes for working families (as in Rochester).

The Highland Park Illinois Community Land Trust preserved this 3-bedroom, 2-bath bungalow for a low-income family.

Another Strength of CLTs: Preventing Foreclosures

The municipal rationale for supporting CLTs has long focused on permanent affordability—the model's effectiveness in ensuring that homes made affordable today will remain affordable tomorrow. Until recently, much less attention has been paid to permanent responsibility i.e., the CLT's durable commitment to backstop the security and success of its first-time homeowners.

The mounting crisis in the U.S. mortgage market has turned the spotlight toward the latter aspect of stewardship. In December 2007, the National Community Land Trust Network surveyed 49 CLTs (nearly a quarter of the nation's total), evaluating the number of mortgage defaults and foreclosures in their portfolios from the time of their founding to the present. Within this small but typical subpopulation of 3,115 residential mortgages, CLTs had intervened 108 times to cure a default before it could result in foreclosure. Nationally, there were only 19 reported cases of foreclosure or transfer of a deed in lieu of foreclosure, a foreclosure rate of 0.6 percent over the entire organizational lifetime of the CLTs. In only 12 of these foreclosures did a lower-income homeowner actually lose his or her home, and in just three cases was a foreclosed property eventually lost from a CLT's portfolio.

In other situations, CLT organizers only reluctantly became housing developers after concluding they had no other choice. In Gloucester, Albany, and Cincinnati, for example, private developers were not building anything that residents could afford and nonprofit developers were doing little to fill the gap. The CLTs saw no other way to serve their communities than to be developers of last resort.

In several other cities, including Portland, Cleveland, and Boston, CLTs had originally intended to confine their activities to stewardship. Existing community development corporations were supposed to be responsible for development, and the CLTs were to preserve the long-term affordability of whatever housing was created. In reality, this seldom happened and the CLTs had to do more development than they had intended.

Whether by choice or by default, real estate development is likely to remain a CLT activity. Nevertheless, a countertrend is emerging as a number of newer CLTs confine their activities to managing land and the affordable housing stock. The CLT-as-steward is slowly becoming a more prominent part of the national landscape.

Indeed, CLTs are being pushed in this direction by the need to distinguish themselves from other nonprofit developers of affordable housing in what has become, in some jurisdictions, a very crowded field. Instead of competing for project subsidies, some CLTs have found a more sustainable niche by specializing in stewardship, an activity that other nonprofits are less willing or less suited to do.

The Montano–Pero family bought their first home in the Hawk Ridge Development of the Northern Communities Land Trust in Duluth, Minnesota.

In other jurisdictions, CLTs are being pulled toward stewardship by the vacuum created by a seismic shift in public policy. Municipal funding for affordable housing—and municipal mandates or incentives for inclusionary housing—once focused almost exclusively on the front end of the development process. It seemed achievement enough to expand the supply of affordably priced or affordably financed housing, with little concern for what happened to the occupancy, condition, and affordability of the homes after they were purchased.

This is no longer the prevailing attitude. Municipal officials have increasingly come to accept the policy prescription that, when public assets or public powers are used to create affordably priced, owner-occupied housing, something must be done to preserve those units for lower-income people for years to come. A growing number of local governments have also recognized that the CLT is one of the most effective and sustainable options for monitoring and enforcing long-term controls over the use and resale of publicly assisted owner-occupied housing.

Of course, serving as a municipality's designated steward is not without challenges. As CLTs discovered in the past when they agreed to leave development entirely in the hands of local community development corporations, allowing others to control the property pipeline can sometimes result in the CLT receiving only a trickle of land and housing—or only those assets no one else wants. Furthermore, when CLTs are not involved in the process of designing and developing the homes, they can find themselves marketing, managing, and stewarding a product no one wants to buy.

Getting government to pay for stewardship can be an even more serious obstacle. Public officials at all levels tend to be more receptive to covering the costs of constructing and financing owner-occupied housing than to covering the costs of monitoring the occupancy, maintaining the condition, and managing the resale of the units once they are built. If CLTs are to forego the fees they now receive from developing housing, they must find other sources of revenue to cover their stewardship costs—either operating subsidies provided by local government or internal fees generated by their own portfolios.

Concentrating on stewardship requires no recasting of the classic CLT. In fact, it might be argued that stewardship, not development, is what the CLT model was always about. The evolving municipal roles in instigating and governing CLTs stretch the model beyond the boundaries within which it was initially conceived and structured. But the role of steward draws the CLT back to its original mission of shepherding resources that a community invests and of capturing values that a community creates. Making stewardship its principal activity brings the model full circle, refocusing the CLT on what it does best.

REFERENCES & RESOURCES

Abromowitz, David M. 2000. An essay on community land trusts: Toward permanently affordable housing. In *Property and values*, Charles Geisler and Gail Daneker, eds. Washington, DC: Island Press.

Cohen, Helen. 1994. Diminishing returns: A critical look at subsidy recapture. In *The affordable city: Toward a third sector housing policy*, J. E. Davis, ed. Philadelphia, PA: Temple University Press.

Davis, John Emmeus. 2006. *Shared equity homeownership: The changing landscape of resale-restricted, owner-occupied housing*. Montclair, NJ: National Housing Institute. *www.nhi.org*

————. 2007. Starting a community land trust: Organizational and operational choices. *www.burlingtonassociates.com*.

Davis, John Emmeus, and Amy Demetrowitz. 2003. *Permanently affordable homeownership: Does the community land trust deliver on its promises?* Burlington, VT: Burlington Community Land Trust. *www.burlingtonassociates.com*

Davis, John Emmeus, Rick Jacobus, and Maureen Hickey. 2008. *Building better city-CLT partnerships: A program manual for municipalities and community land trusts*. Working Paper. Cambridge, MA: Lincoln Institute of Land Policy.

Institute for Community Economics. 1972. *The community land trust: A guide to a new model for land tenure in America*. Cambridge, MA: Center for Community Economic Development.

————. 1982. *The community land trust handbook*. Emmaus, PA: Rodale Press.

————. 2002. *The community land trust legal manual*. Springfield, MA: Institute for Community Economics.

Herman, Kim. 2006. Community land trusts come of age. *Washington State Housing Finance Commission executive director's newsletter. www.wshfc. org/newsletter*

Jacobus, Rick, and Amy Cohen. Forthcoming. Creating permanently affordable homeownership through community land trusts. In *California affordable housing*, Rob Weiner and Neal Richman, eds. Point Arena, CA: Solano Press.

Jacobus, Rick, and Jeffrey Lubell. 2007. Preservation of affordable homeownership: A continuum of strategies. Policy brief. Washington, DC: Center for Housing Policy.

McKenzie, Tim. 2007. The case for plan B. *Shelterforce* 24:151.

Robinson, Carla J. 2008. *Valuation and taxation of resale-restricted, owner-occupied housing*. Working Paper. Cambridge, MA: Lincoln Institute of Land Policy.

Sungu-Eryilmaz, Yesim, and Rosalind Greenstein. 2007. *A national study of community land trusts*. Working Paper. Cambridge, MA: Lincoln Institute of Land Policy.

Web Resources

Burlington Associates in Community Development CLT Resource Center
www.burlingtonassociates.com

E.F. Schumacher Society
www.schumachersociety.org

Equity Trust, Inc.
www.equitytrust.org

National Community Land Trust Network
www.cltnetwork.org

National Housing Conference
www.nhc.org/housing/sharedequity

National Housing Institute
www.nhi.org

Video Resources

Chasnoff, Deborah, and Helen Cohen. 1998. *Homes & hands: Community land trusts in action*. Produced for the Institute for Community Economics by Women's Educational Media, distributed by New Day Films, Hohokus, NJ. *www.newday.com*

Mahan, Leah, and Mark Lipman. 1996. *Holding ground: The rebirth of Dudley Street*. Distributed by New Day Films, Hohokus, NJ. *www.newday.com*

NCB Capital Impact and NeighborWorks America. 2007. *A new way home: Sharing equity to build wealth*. Produced by Hare in the Gate Productions. *www.ncbcapitalimpact.org*

ACKNOWLEDGMENTS

This report has benefited immeasurably from the close and critical reading of earlier drafts by several colleagues, including Julie Brunner, Michael Brown, Lisa Byers, Tad Everhart, Roz Greenstein, Greg Rosenberg, and Kirby White. Their comments helped us sharpen our recommendations and correct many errors of fact or tone. Any confusions or mistakes that remain are, of course, the responsibility of the authors alone.

We especially wish to acknowledge the many contributions of our research associate, Maureen Hickey, who arranged, conducted, and summarized the many phone interviews that inform this report. In addition, Maureen took on the arduous task of collecting and reviewing dozens of grant agreements, loan documents, and similar contracts that form the legal framework for city–CLT partnerships across the United States. As we sifted through our findings, weighing which ways of supporting a CLT might merit being mentioned as a model practice, Maureen helped to keep us grounded in the materials she had collected on our behalf.

We are grateful to Roz Greenstein and the Lincoln Institute of Land Policy for their support of this work, and to Marcia Fernald for her careful, thoughtful, and respectful editing of this policy focus report.

We also recognize the CLT practitioners and municipal officials who shared their experiences and are listed below.

CLT Practitioners
Dena Al-Khatib, Chicago Community Land Trust, Illinois
Lisa Byers, OPAL Community Land Trust, Orcus Island, Washington
Connie Chavez, Sawmill Community Land Trust, Albuquerque, New Mexico
Amy Demetrowitz, Champlain Housing Trust, Burlington, Vermont
Martina Guilfoil, Community Housing Trust of Sarasota County, Florida
Alison Handler, Portland Community Land Trust, Oregon
Roger Lewis and Aaron Miripol, Thistle Community Housing, Boulder, Colorado
Marge Misak, Cuyahoga Community Land Trust, Cleveland, Ohio
Steve Ostiguy, Church Community Housing, Newport, Rhode Island
Greg Rosenberg, Madison Area Community Land Trust, Wisconsin
Paul Schissler, Kulshan Community Land Trust, Bellingham, Washington
Mary Ellen Tamasy, Highland Park Illinois Community Land Trust
Jeff Washburne, City of Lakes Community Land Trust, Minneapolis, Minnesota
Jason Webb, Dudley Neighbors, Inc., Boston, Massachusetts
Christine Westfall, Orange Community Housing and Land Trust, Carrboro, North Carolina
Dave Wilkinson, City First Enterprises, Washington, DC
Ian Winters, Northern California Community Land Trust, Berkeley, California

Municipal Officials
Trell Anderson, Clackamas County, Oregon (formerly with City of Portland)
Loryn Clarke, Town of Chapel Hill, North Carolina
John Feuerbach, City of Boston, Massachusetts
Joe Gray, Delray Beach Community Redevelopment Authority, Florida
Hickory Hurie, City of Madison, Wisconsin
Marti Luick, City of Albuquerque, New Mexico
Brian Pine, City of Burlington, Vermont
Lee Smith, City of Highland Park, Illinois
Jeff Yegian, City of Boulder, Colorado